••⊙• *BULLETPOINTS* •⊙•••

PLANETS

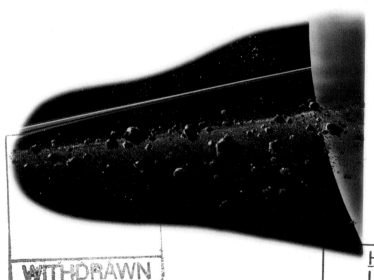

John Farndon
Consultant: Tim Furniss

MiLes
KeLLy
PUBLISHING

First published in 2004 by Miles Kelly Publishing Ltd
Bardfield Centre, Great Bardfield
Essex, CM7 4SL

2 4 6 8 10 9 7 5 3 1

Editor: Belinda Gallagher

Design: Andy Knight

Picture Research: Liberty Newton

Production: Estela Godoy

British Library Cataloguing-in-Publication Data
A catalogue record for this book is available from the British Library

ISBN 1-84236-374-3

Printed in China

www.mileskelly.net
info@mileskelly.net

The publishers would like to thank the following artists who have contributed to this book:
Kuo Kang Chen, Rob Jakeway, Janos Marffy, Rob Sheffield, Mike White

Contents

The Earth

- **The Earth is the third planet** out from the Sun, 149.6 million km away on average. On 3 January, at the nearest point of its orbit (called the perihelion), the Earth is 147,097,800 km away from the Sun. On 4 July, at its furthest (the aphelion), it is 152,098,200 km away.

- **The Earth is the fifth largest planet** in the Solar System, with a diameter of 12,756 km and a circumference of 40,024 km at the Equator.

- **The Earth is one of four rocky planets,** along with Mercury, Venus and Mars. It is made mostly of rock, with a core of iron and nickel.

- **No other planet in the solar system** has water on its surface, which is why Earth is uniquely suitable for life. Over 70% of Earth's surface is under water.

- **The Earth's atmosphere** is mainly harmless nitrogen and life-giving oxygen, and it is over 700 km deep. The oxygen has been made and maintained by plants over billions of years.

- **The Earth formed 4.65 billion years** ago from clouds of space dust whirling around the young Sun. The planet was so hot that it was molten at first. Only slowly did the surface cool into a hard crust.

▲ *The Earth from space. It is the only planet known to support life.*

- **The Earth's orbit** around the Sun is 939,886,400 km long and takes 365.242 days.

- **The Earth is tilted** at an angle of 23.5°. Even so, it orbits the Sun in a level plane, called the plane of the ecliptic.

- **The Earth is made up** of the same basic materials as meteorites and the other rocky planets – mostly iron (35%), oxygen (28%), magnesium (17%), silicon (13%) and nickel (2.7%).

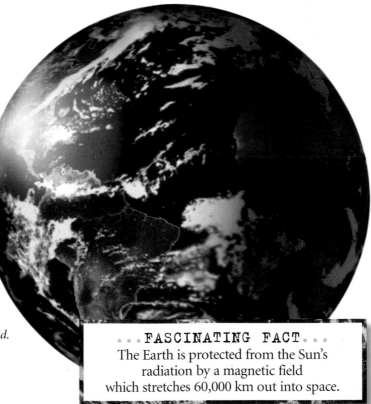

▶ *Most of the Earth's rocky crust is drowned beneath oceans, formed from steam belched out by volcanoes early in the planet's history. The Earth is just the right distance from the Sun for surface temperatures to stay an average 15°C, and keep most of its water liquid.*

> ...**FASCINATING FACT**...
> The Earth is protected from the Sun's radiation by a magnetic field which stretches 60,000 km out into space.

Atmosphere

- **An atmosphere** is the gases held around a planet by its gravity.

- **Every planet in the Solar System** has an atmosphere.

- **Each atmosphere** is very different. Earth's atmosphere is the only one humans can breathe.

- **Atmospheres** are not fixed, but can change rapidly.

- **Moons** are generally too small and their gravity is too weak to hold on to an atmosphere. But some moons in the solar system have one, including Saturn's moon Titan.

- **The primordial (earliest) atmospheres** came from the swirling cloud of gas and dust surrounding the young Sun.

- **If Earth and the other rocky planets** had primordial atmospheres, they were stripped away by the solar wind.

- **Earth's atmosphere** was formed first from gases pouring out of volcanoes.

- **Jupiter's atmosphere** is partly primordial, but it has been altered by the Sun's radiation, and the planet's own internal heat and lightning storms.

◀ *Earth's unique atmosphere shields us from the Sun's dangerous rays, as well as giving us oxygen and water.*

▼ *Smoking volcano on the Pacific island of Hawaii. Volcano gases helped to form the Earth's atmosphere.*

Planets

- **Planets** are globe-shaped space objects that orbit a star.

- **Planets begin life** at the same time as their star, from the left over clouds of gas and dust.

- **Planets are never** more than 20% of the size of their star. If they were bigger, they would have become stars.

- **Some planets,** called terrestrial planets, have a surface of solid rock. Others, called gas planets, have a surface of liquid or airy gas.

- **The solar system** has nine planets including Pluto. But Pluto may be an escaped moon or an asteroid, not a planet.

- **Giant planets** have now been detected orbiting stars other than the Sun. These are called extra-solar planets.

- **Extra-solar planets** are too far away to see, but can be detected because they make their star wobble.

- **One extra-solar planet** has now been photographed.

- **Among the nine stars** so far known to have planets are 47 Ursae Majoris, 51 Pegasi, and 70 Virginis.

- **Four of the new planets** – called 51 Peg planets, after the planet that circles 51 Pegasi – seem to orbit their stars in less than 15 days. The planet orbiting Tau Bootis gets around in just 3.3 days!

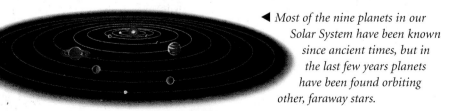

◀ *Most of the nine planets in our Solar System have been known since ancient times, but in the last few years planets have been found orbiting other, faraway stars.*

▲ *The planets of our Solar System: from the front, Neptune, Uranus, Saturn, Jupiter, Mars, Earth and its moon, Venus and Mercury. Pluto (not shown) is the furthest out from the Sun.*

Mercury

- **Mercury is the nearest planet** to the Sun – during its orbit it is between 45.9 and 69.7 million km away.

- **Mercury is the fastest orbiting** of all the planets, getting around the Sun in just 88 days.

- **Mercury takes 58.6 days** to rotate once, so a Mercury day lasts nearly 59 times as long as ours.

- **Temperatures** on Mercury veer from -180°C at night to over 430°C during the day (enough to melt lead).

- **The crust and mantle** are made largely of rock, but the core (75% of its diameter) is solid iron.

- **Mercury's dusty surface** is pocketed by craters made by space debris crashing into it.

▲ *Mercury is a tiny planet with a thin atmosphere and a solid core.*

- **With barely 20% of Earth's mass,** Mercury is so small that its gravity can only hold on to a very thin atmosphere of sodium vapour.

- **Mercury is so small** that its core has cooled and become solid (unlike Earth's). As this happened, Mercury shrank and its surface wrinkled like the skin of an old apple.

- **Craters on Mercury** discovered by the USA's *Mariner* space probe have names like Bach, Beethoven, Wagner, Shakespeare and Tolstoy.

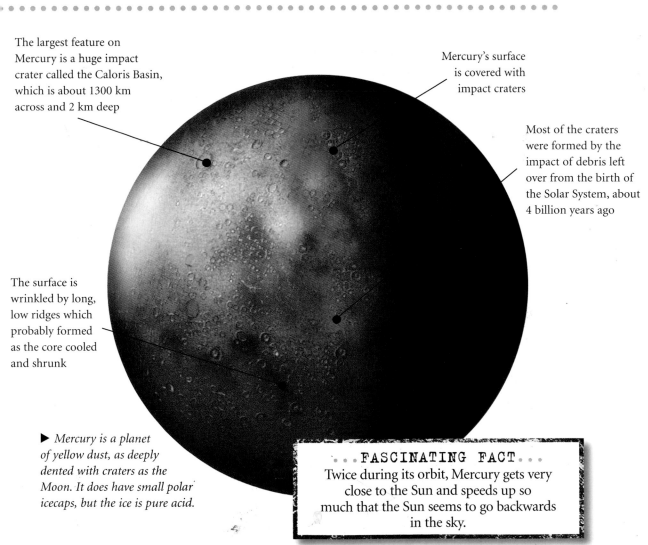

The largest feature on Mercury is a huge impact crater called the Caloris Basin, which is about 1300 km across and 2 km deep

Mercury's surface is covered with impact craters

Most of the craters were formed by the impact of debris left over from the birth of the Solar System, about 4 billion years ago

The surface is wrinkled by long, low ridges which probably formed as the core cooled and shrunk

▶ Mercury is a planet of yellow dust, as deeply dented with craters as the Moon. It does have small polar icecaps, but the ice is pure acid.

...FASCINATING FACT...
Twice during its orbit, Mercury gets very close to the Sun and speeds up so much that the Sun seems to go backwards in the sky.

Venus

- **Venus** is the second planet out from the Sun – its orbit makes it 107.4 million km away at its nearest and 109 million km away at its furthest.

- **Venus shines like a star** in the night sky because its thick atmosphere reflects sunlight amazingly well. This planet is the brightest thing in the sky, after the Sun and the Moon.

- **Venus is called the Evening Star** because it can be seen from Earth in the evening, just after sunset. It can also be seen before sunrise, though. It is visible at these times because it is quite close to the Sun.

- **Venus's cloudy atmosphere** is a thick mixture of carbon dioxide gas and sulphuric acid.

- **Venus is the hottest planet** in the Solar System, with a surface temperature of over 470°C.

- **Venus is so hot** because the carbon dioxide in its atmosphere works like the panes of glass in a greenhouse to trap the Sun's heat. This overheating is called a runaway greenhouse effect.

- **Venus's thick clouds** hide its surface so well that until space probes detected the very high temperatures some people thought there might be jungles beneath the clouds.

▲ *This is a view of a 6 km-high volcano on Venus' surface called Maat Mons. It is not an actual photograph, but was created on computer from radar data collected by the Magellan orbiter, which reached Venus in the 1980s. The colours are what astronomers guess them to be from their knowledge of the chemistry of Venus.*

- **Venus's day** (the time it takes to spin round once) lasts 243 Earth days – longer than its year, which lasts 224.7 days. But because Venus rotates backwards, the Sun actually comes up twice during the planet's yearly orbit – once every 116.8 days.

- **Venus is the nearest** of all the planets to Earth in size, measuring 12,102 km across its diameter.

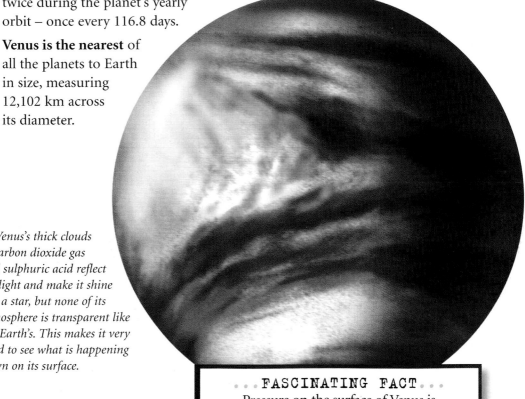

▶ *Venus's thick clouds of carbon dioxide gas and sulphuric acid reflect sunlight and make it shine like a star, but none of its atmosphere is transparent like the Earth's. This makes it very hard to see what is happening down on its surface.*

> ...FASCINATING FACT...
> Pressure on the surface of Venus is
> 90 times greater than that on Earth!

13

Mars

- **Mars** is the nearest planet to Earth after Venus, and it is the only planet to have either an atmosphere or a daytime temperature close to ours.

- **Mars is called the red planet** because of its rusty red colour. This comes from oxidized (rusted) iron in its soil.

- **Mars is the fourth planet** out from the Sun, orbiting it at an average distance of 227.9 million km. It takes 687 days to complete its orbit.

- **Mars is 6786 km** in diameter and spins round once every 24.62 hours – almost the same time as the Earth takes to rotate.

- **Mars's volcano Olympus Mons** is the biggest in the Solar System. It covers the same area as Ireland and is three times higher than Mount Everest.

- **In the 1880s,** the American astronomer Percival Lowell was convinced that the dark lines he could see on Mars' surface through his telescope were canals built by Martians.

- **The *Viking* probes** found no evidence of life on Mars, but the discovery of a possible fossil of a micro-organism in a Mars rock means the hunt for life on Mars is on. Future missions to the planet will hunt for life below its surface.

- **The evidence is growing** that Mars was warmer and wetter in the past, although scientists cannot say how much water there was, or when and why it dried up.

▲ *Mars' surface is cracked by a valley called the Vallis Marineris – so big it makes the Grand Canyon look tiny.*

● **Mars has two tiny moons** called Phobos and Deimos. Phobos is just 27 km across, while Deimos is just 15 km across and has so little gravity that you could reach escape velocity riding a bike up a ramp!

▶ *Mars is the best known planet besides Earth, studied by countless astronomers through powerful telescopes, scanned by orbiting space probes, and landed on more times than any other planet. All this effort has revealed a planet with a surface like a red, rocky desert – but there is also plenty of evidence that Mars wasn't always so desert-like.*

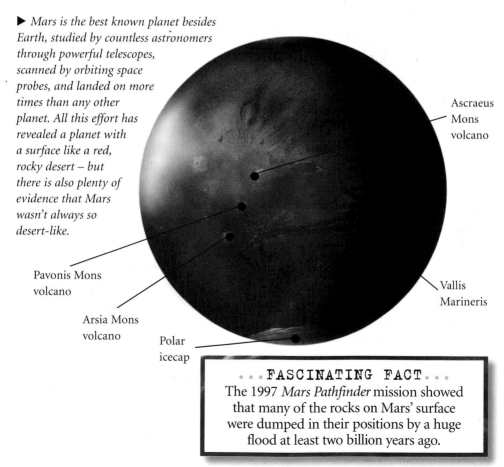

Ascraeus
Mons
volcano

Pavonis Mons
volcano

Vallis
Marineris

Arsia Mons
volcano

Polar
icecap

FASCINATING FACT
The 1997 *Mars Pathfinder* mission showed that many of the rocks on Mars' surface were dumped in their positions by a huge flood at least two billion years ago.

Mars landing

- **In the 1970s** the US *Vikings 1* and *2* and the Soviet *Mars 3* and *5* probes all reached the surface of Mars.

- *Mars 3* was the first probe to make a soft landing on Mars, on 2 December 1971, and sent back data for 20 seconds before it unexpectedly fell silent.

- *Viking 1* sent back the first colour pictures from Mars, on 26 July 1976.

- **The aim of the *Viking* missions** was to find signs of life, but there were none. Even so, the *Viking* landers sent back plenty of information about the geology and atmosphere of Mars.

- **On 4 July 1997,** the US *Mars Pathfinder* probe arrived on Mars and at once began beaming back 'live' TV pictures from the planet's surface.

- *Mars Pathfinder* used air bags to cushion its landing on the planet's surface.

- **Two days after** the *Pathfinder* landed, it sent out a wheeled robot vehicle called the *Sojourner* to survey the surrounding area.

- **The *Sojourner*** showed a rock-strewn plain which looks as if it were once swept by floods.

- *Pathfinder* and *Sojourner* operated for 83 days and took more than 16,000 photos.

- **Missions to Mars** early in the 21st century may include the first return flight after 2010.

▶ *The* Mars Pathfinder *mission provided many stunning images of the surface of the 'red planet', many taken by the* Sojourner *as it motored over the surface.*

Jupiter

- **Jupiter** is the biggest planet in the Solar System – twice as heavy as all the other planets put together.

- **Jupiter has no surface** for a spacecraft to land on because it is made mostly from helium gas and hydrogen. The massive pull of Jupiter's gravity squeezes the hydrogen so hard that it is liquid.

- **Towards Jupiter's core,** immense pressure turns the hydrogen to solid metal.

- **The Ancient Greeks** originally named the planet Zeus, after the king of their gods. Jupiter was the Romans' name for Zeus.

- **Jupiter spins right round** in less than ten hours, which means that the planet's surface is moving at nearly 50,000 km/h.

- **Jupiter's speedy spin makes** its middle bulge out. It also churns up the planet's metal core until it generates a hugely powerful magnetic field ten times as strong as the Earth's.

- **Jupiter has a Great Red Spot** – a huge swirl of red clouds measuring more than 40,000 km across. The scientist Robert Hooke first noticed the spot in 1644.

- **Jupiter's four biggest moons** were first spotted by Galileo in the 17th century (see Jupiter's Galilean moons). Their names are Io, Europa, Callisto and Ganymede.

- **Jupiter also has 17 smaller moons** – Metis, Adastrea, Amalthea, Thebe, Leda, Himalia, Lysithea, Elara, Ananke, Carme, Pasiphaë, Sinope as well as five recent discoveries.

- **Jupiter is so massive** that the pressure at its heart makes it glow very faintly with invisible infrared rays. Indeed, it glows as brightly as four million billion 100-watt light bulbs. But it is not quite big enough for nuclear reactions to start, and make it become a star.

▼ *Jupiter is a gigantic planet, 142,984 km across. Its orbit takes 11.86 years and varies between 740.9 and 815.7 million km from the Sun. Its surface is often rent by huge lightning flashes and thunderclaps, and temperatures here plunge to -150°C. Looking at Jupiter's surface, all you can see is a swirling mass of red, brown and yellow clouds of ammonia, including the Great Red Spot.*

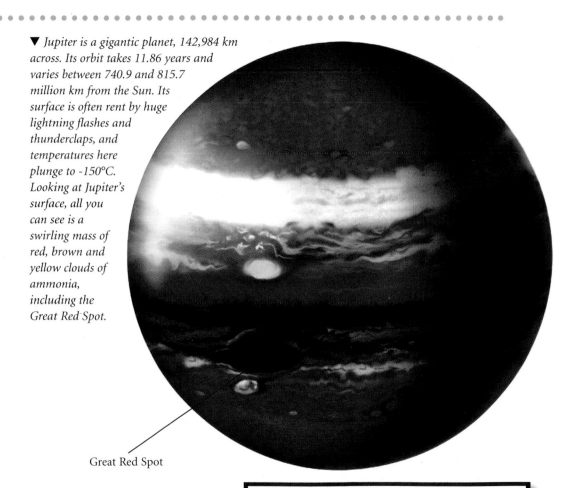

Great Red Spot

...FASCINATING FACT...
The Galileo space probe reached Jupiter
and its moons in the year 1995.

Jupiter's Galilean moons

- **The Galilean moons** are the four biggest of Jupiter's moons. They were discovered by Galileo, centuries before astronomers identified the other, smaller ones.

- **Ganymede is the biggest** of the Galilean moons – at 5268 km across, it is larger than the planet Mercury.

- **Ganymede looks hard** but under its shell of solid ice is 900 km of slushy, half-melted ice and water.

Io

- **Callisto is the second biggest,** at 4806 km across.

- **Callisto is scarred** with craters from bombardments early in the Solar System's life.

Europa

- **Io is the third biggest,** at 3642 km across.

- **Io's surface is a mass of volcanoes,** caused by it being stretched and squeezed by Jupiter's massive gravity.

- **The smallest** of the Galilean moons is Europa, at 3138 km across.

- **Europa is covered in ice** and looks like a shiny, honey-coloured billiard ball from a distance – but a close-up view reveals countless cracks in its surface.

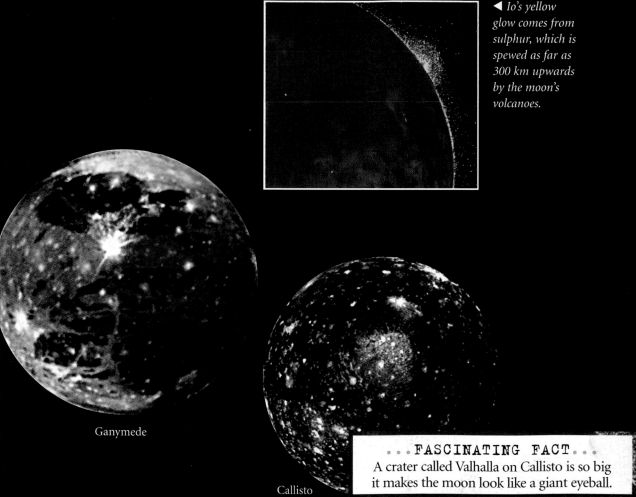

◄ Io's yellow glow comes from sulphur, which is spewed as far as 300 km upwards by the moon's volcanoes.

Ganymede

Callisto

...FASCINATING FACT...
A crater called Valhalla on Callisto is so big
it makes the moon look like a giant eyeball.

Saturn

- **Saturn is the second biggest planet** in the Solar System – 815 times as big in volume as the Earth, and measuring 120,000 km around its equator.

- **Saturn takes 29 and a half years** to travel round the Sun, so Saturn's year is 29.46 Earth years. The planet's complete orbit is a journey of more than 4.5 billion km.

- **Winds ten times stronger than** a hurricane on Earth swirl around Saturn's equator, reaching up to 1,100 km/h – and they never let up, even for a moment.

- **Saturn is named after Saturnus,** the Ancient Roman god of seed-time and harvest. He was celebrated in the Roman's wild, Christmas-time festival of Saturnalia.

- **Saturn is not solid,** but is made almost entirely of gas – mostly liquid hydrogen and helium. Only in the planet's very small core is there any solid rock.

- **Because Saturn is so massive,** the pressure at its heart is enough to turn hydrogen solid. That is why there is a layer of metallic hydrogen around the planet's inner core of rock.

- **Saturn is one of the fastest spinning** of all the planets. Despite its size, it rotates in just 11.5 hours – which means it turns round at over 10,000 km/h.

Saturn's rings are made of many millions of tiny, ice-coated rock fragments

- **Saturn's surface appears** to be almost completely smooth, though *Voyager 1* and *2* did photograph a few small, swirling storms when they flew past.

- **Saturn has a very powerful magnetic field** and sends out strong radio signals.

◄ *Saturn is the queen of the planets. Almost as big as Jupiter, and made largely of liquid hydrogen and helium, Saturn is stunningly beautiful, with its smooth, pale-butterscotch surface (clouds of ammonia) and its shimmering halo of rings. But it is a very secretive planet. Telescopes have never pierced its upper atmosphere, and data from the fly-bys of the* Voyager *probes focused on its rings and moons. But the Cassini probe, launched in 1997, may change this when it eventually descends into Saturn's atmosphere.*

...**FASCINATING FACT**...
Saturn is so low in density that if you could find a bath big enough, you would be able to float the planet in the water.

Saturn's rings

- **Saturn's rings** are sets of thin rings of ice, dust and tiny rocks, which orbit the planet around its equator.

- **The rings shimmer** as their ice is caught by sunlight.

- **The rings** may be fragments of a moon that was torn apart by Saturn's gravity before it formed properly.

- **Galileo was first** to see Saturn's rings, in 1610. But it was Dutch scientist Christian Huygens (1629-95) who first realized they were rings, in 1659.

- **There are two** main sets of rings – the A and the B rings.

- **The A and B rings** are separated by a gap called the Cassini division, after Italian astronomer Jean Cassini (1625-1712), who spotted it in 1675.

▲ *Saturn's rings are one of the wonders of the Solar System, and many people think they make it the most beautiful planet.*

- **A third large ring** called the C or crepe ring was spotted closer to the planet in 1850.

- **In the 1980s,** space probes revealed many other rings and 10,000 or more ringlets, some just 10 m wide.

- **The rings are** (in order out from the planet) D, C, B, Cassini division, A, F, G and E. The A ring has its own gap called the Encke division.

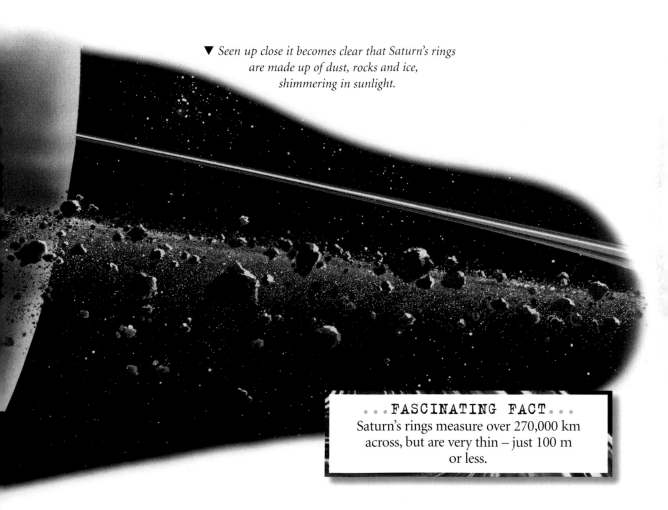

▼ *Seen up close it becomes clear that Saturn's rings are made up of dust, rocks and ice, shimmering in sunlight.*

...FASCINATING FACT...
Saturn's rings measure over 270,000 km across, but are very thin – just 100 m or less.

Uranus

- **Uranus is the seventh planet** out from the Sun. Its orbit keeps it 1784 million km away on average and takes 84 years to complete.

- **Uranus tilts so far on its side** that it seems to roll around the Sun like a gigantic bowling ball. The angle of its tilt is 98°, in fact, so its equator runs top to bottom. This tilt may be the result of a collision with a meteor or another planet a long time ago.

- **In summer on Uranus,** the Sun does not set for 20 years. In winter, darkness lasts for over 20 years. In autumn, the Sun rises and sets every nine hours.

- **Uranus has 17 moons,** all named after characters in William Shakespeare's plays. There are five large moons – Ariel, Umbriel, Titania, Oberon and Miranda. The ten smaller ones were discovered by the *Voyager 2* space probe in 1986.

- **Uranus' moon Miranda** is the weirdest moon of all. It seems to have been blasted apart, then put itself back together again!

- **Because Uranus is so far from the Sun,** it is very, very cold, with surface temperatures dropping to -210°C. Sunlight takes just eight minutes to reach Earth, but 2.5 hours to reach Uranus.

- **Uranus' icy atmosphere** is made of hydrogen and helium. Winds whistle around the planet at over 2000 km/h – ten times as fast as hurricanes on Earth.

Uranus has its own, very faint set of rings

- **Uranus' surface** is an ice-cold ocean of liquid methane (natural gas), thousands of kilometres deep, which gives the planet its beautiful colour. If you fell into this ocean even for a fraction of a second, you would freeze so hard that you would shatter like glass.

- **Uranus is only faintly visible** from Earth. It looks no bigger than a star through a telescope, and was not identified until 1781.

- **Uranus was named** after Urania, the ancient Greek goddess of astronomy.

Uranus has an atmosphere of hydrogen and helium gas

The planet's surface of liquid methane gives it a stunning blue colour

◀ *Uranus is the third largest planet in the Solar System – 51,118 km across and with a mass 14.54 times that of the Earth's. The planet spins round once every 17.24 hours but because it is lying almost on its side, this has almost no effect on the length of its day. Instead, this depends on where the planet is in its orbit of the Sun. Like Saturn, Uranus has rings, but they are much thinner and were only detected in 1977. They are made of the darkest material in the Solar System.*

. . . FASCINATING FACT . . .
On Uranus in spring, the Sun sets every
nine hours – backwards!

Neptune

- **Neptune is the eighth** planet out from the Sun, varying in distance from 4456 to 4537 million km.

- **Neptune was discovered** in 1846 because two mathematicians, John Couch Adams in England and Urbain le Verrier in France, worked out that it must be there because of the effect of its gravity on the movement of Uranus.

- **Neptune is so far** from the Sun that its orbit lasts 164.79 Earth years. Indeed, it has not yet completed one orbit since it was discovered in 1846.

- **Like Uranus,** Neptune has a surface of icy cold liquid methane (-210°C), and an atmosphere of hydrogen and helium.

- **Unlike Uranus,** which is almost perfectly blue, Neptune has white clouds, created by heat inside the planet.

- **Neptune has the strongest winds** in the Solar System, blowing at up to 700 m per second.

- **Neptune has eight moons,** each named after characters from ancient Greek myths – Naiad, Thalassa, Despoina, Galatea, Larissa, Proteus, Triton and Nereid.

- **Neptune's moon Triton** looks like a green melon, while its icecaps of frozen nitrogen look like pink ice cream. It also has volcanoes that erupt fountains of ice.

- **Triton is the only moon** to orbit backwards.

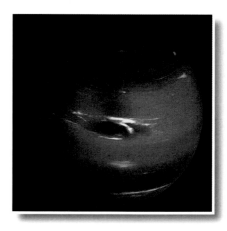

▲ *This photo of Neptune was taken by the* Voyager 2 *spacecraft in 1989. The Great Dark Spot, and the little white tail of clouds, named Scooter by astronomers, are both clearly visible.*

▼ *Neptune is the fourth largest planet. At 49,528 km across, it is slightly smaller than Uranus – but it is actually a little heavier. Like Uranus, its oceans of incredibly cold liquid methane make it a beautiful shiny blue, although Neptune's surface is a deeper blue than that of Uranus. Again like Uranus, Neptune has a thin layer of rings. But Neptune's are level, and not at right angles to the Sun. Neptune has a Great Dark Spot, like Jupiter's Great Red Spot, where storms whip up swirling clouds.*

Great Dark Spot

...**FASCINATING FACT**...
Neptune's moon Triton is the coldest place
in the Solar System, with surface
temperatures of -236°C.

Pluto

- **Pluto was the last** of all the planets to be discovered, and it was only found because it has a slight effect on the orbits of Neptune and Uranus.

- **Pluto is the furthest out** of all the planets, varying from 4730 to 7375 million km from the Sun.

- **The Sun is so far from Pluto** that if you could stand on the planet's surface, the Sun would look no bigger than a star in Earth's sky and shine no more brightly than the Moon does.

- **Pluto's orbit** is so far from the Sun that it takes 248.54 years just to travel right around once. This means that a year on Pluto lasts almost three Earth centuries. A day, however, lasts just under a week.

- **Pluto has a strange elliptical (oval) orbit** which actually brings it closer to the Sun than Neptune for a year or two every few centuries.

- **Unlike all the other planets** which orbit on exactly the same plane (level) as the Earth, Pluto's orbit cuts across diagonally.

- **While studying** a photo of Pluto in 1978, American astronomer James Christy noticed a bump. This turned out to be a large moon, which was later named Charon.

- **Charon** is about half the size of Pluto and they orbit one another, locked together like a weightlifter's dumbbells.

- **Charon** always stays in the same place in Pluto's sky, looking three times as big as our Moon.

▲ *Pluto is tiny in comparison to the Earth, which is why it was so hard to find. Earth is five times bigger and 500 times as heavy. This illustration shows the relative sizes of the Earth and Pluto.*

● **Unlike the other outer planets,** Pluto is made from rock. But the rock is covered in water, ice and a thin layer of frozen methane.

Daytime temperatures on Pluto's surface are -220°C or less, so the surface is thought to be coated in frozen methane.

▶ *This picture of Pluto is entirely imaginary, since it is so small and so far away that even photographs from the Hubble space telescope show no more detail on Pluto's surface than you could see on the surface of a billiard ball. However, a twinkling of starlight around the edge of the planet shows that it must have some kind of atmosphere.*

...**FASCINATING FACT**...
Pluto was discovered on 18 February 1930 by young American astronomer Clyde Tombaugh.

Asteroids

- **Asteroids** are lumps of rock that orbit the Sun. They are sometimes called the minor planets.

- **Most asteroids** are in the Asteroid Belt, which lies between Mars and Jupiter.

- **Some distant asteroids** are made of ice and orbit the Sun beyond Neptune.

- **A few asteroids** come near the Earth. These are called Near Earth Objects (NEOs).

- **The first asteroid to be discovered** was Ceres in 1801. It was detected by Giuseppi Piazzi, one of the Celestial Police whose mission was to find a 'missing' planet.

- **Ceres** is the biggest asteroid – 940 km across, and 0.0002% the size of the Earth.

- **The *Galileo* space probe** took close-up pictures of the asteroids Ida and Gaspra in 1991 and 1993.

- **There are half a million or so** asteroids bigger than 1 km across. More than 200 asteroids are over 100 km across.

- **The Trojan asteroids** are groups of asteroids that follow the same orbit as Jupiter. Many are named after warriors in the ancient Greek tales of the Trojan wars.

Jupiter

Mars

▲ *Most asteroids – more than half a million – orbit the Sun in the Asteroid Belt, between Mars and Jupiter.*

33

Comets

- **Comets are bright objects** with long tails, which we sometimes see streaking across the night sky.

- **They may look spectacular,** but a comet is just a dirty ball of ice a few kilometres across.

- **Many comets orbit the Sun,** but their orbits are very long and they spend most of the time in the far reaches of the Solar System. We see them when their orbit brings them close to the Sun for a few weeks.

- **A comet's tail** is made as it nears the Sun and begins to melt. A vast plume of gas millions of kilometres across is blown out behind by the solar wind. The tail is what you see, shining as the sunlight catches it.

- **Comets called periodics** appear at regular intervals.

- **Some comets reach speeds** of two million km/h as they near the Sun.

- **Far away from the Sun,** comets slow down to 1000 km/h or so – that is why they stay away for so long.

- **The visit of the comet Hale-Bopp** in 1997 gave the brightest view of a comet since 1811, visible even from brightly lit cities.

- **The Shoemaker-Levy 9 comet** smashed into Jupiter in July 1994, with the biggest crash ever witnessed.

- **The most famous comet** of all is Halley's comet.

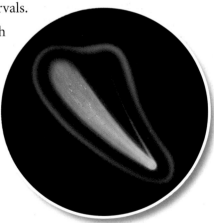

▲ *The tail of a comet always points away from the Sun.*

▶ *Comet Kahoutek streaks through the night sky.*

Halley's comet

- **Halley's comet** is named after the British scientist Edmund Halley (1656-1742).

- **Halley predicted** that this particular comet would return in 1758, 16 years after his death. It was the first time a comet's arrival had been predicted.

- **Halley's comet** orbits the Sun every 76 years.

- **Its orbit** loops between Mercury and Venus, and stretches out beyond Neptune.

- **Halley's comet last** came in sight in 1986. Its next visit will be in 2062.

- **The Chinese** described a visit of Halley's comet as long ago as 240BC.

- **When Halley's comet** was seen in AD837, Chinese astronomers wrote that its head was as bright as Venus and its tail stretched right through the sky.

▲ *The section of the Bayeux tapestry that shows Halley's comet (top, right of centre).*

- **Harold, King of England,** saw the comet in 1066. When he was defeated by William the Conqueror a few months later, people took the comet's visit as an evil omen.

- **Halley's comet** was embroidered on the Bayeux tapestry, which shows Harold's defeat by William.

▲ *The bright head and long tail of Halley's comet.*

...FASCINATING FACT...
Halley's comet was seen in about 8BC, so some say it was the Bible's Star of Bethlehem.

Rotation

- **Rotation is the normal motion** (movement) of most space objects. Rotate means 'spin'.

- **Stars spin,** planets spin, moons spin and galaxies spin – even atoms spin.

- **Moons rotate** around planets, and planets rotate around stars.

- **The Earth rotates** once every 23.93 hours. This is called its rotation period.

- **We do not feel the Earth's rotation** – that it is hurtling around the Sun, while the Sun whizzes around the galaxy – because we are moving with it.

- **Things rotate because** they have kinetic (movement) energy. They cannot fly away because they are held in place by gravity, and the only place they can go is round.

- **The fastest rotating planet** is Saturn, which turns right around once every 10.23 hours.

- **The slowest rotating planet** is Venus, which takes 243.01 days to turn round.

- **The Sun takes 25.4 days** to rotate, but since the Earth is going around it too, it seems to take 27.27 days.

...FASCINATING FACT...
The fastest spinning objects in the
Universe are neutron stars – these can
rotate 500 times in just one second!

▶ Rotating galaxies are
just part of the spinning,
moving Universe.

Index